SOLIDWORKS

FOR BEGINNERS

(New Edition)

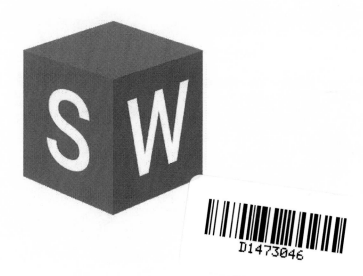

D1473046

ARSATH NATHEEM S

WHY I WROTE THIS BOOK

I wrote this book because SOLIDWORKS is most powerful CAD Modelling software that uses mathematical equations (parametric variables) to fabricate parts starting without help. In case you're anyplace in the design and engineering space, odds are you'll should be "familiar" in SOLIDWORKS. Guessing out how to utilize the instrument effectively is an extraordinarily valuable ability that is a basic thing for the advanced product design and mechanical Designs. It is likewise valuable for the business visionary and additionally little organization to comprehend a combine of the fundamentals, as this will help you have a superior comprehension of what's included with regards to building up your product., this book will help you boost your chance utilizing the software and assemble encounter quicker, the software is essentially a one-stop shop for design so you able to transform ideas into reality.

This book is intended to help beginners take in the necessary ideas of SOLIDWORKS and great solid modeling technique in a simple to learn by doing, This book not only focuses on the utilizations of the devices/commands of SOLIDWORKS yet in addition on the idea of design. Each page of this book contains instructional exercises which educate beginners how things should be possible in SOLIDWORKS step by step. In addition, each part ends with hands-on test drives which enable user to feel themselves the convenience and intense capacities of SOLIDWORKS. To the end of this book, you will have a genuinely great understanding of the SOLIDWORKS interface and the most ordinarily utilized commands for part modeling, assembly and enumerating in the wake of finishing a progression of segments and their 2D illustrations finish with Bill of Materials.

TABLE OF CONTENTS

CHAPTER 1

Introduction

SolidWorks is 3D modeling CAD software which permits users to design a complete solid models in a virtual environment for together design and analysis. In SolidWorks, you can sketch ideas and experimentation with dissimilar designs to make 3D models. SolidWorks Association was established in 1993 by MIT (Massachusetts Institute of Innovation) graduate Hirschtick Jon. By way of indicated by the distributer, more than three million engineers and product designers at in excess of 167,000 companies were utilizing SolidWorks starting at 2013. Additionally, as specified by the company, financial year 2011 to 12 revenue for SolidWorks totaled $483 million. DS Solidworks Corporation, has vended more than 3.7 million licenses of Software around the world.

Basics and Fundamentals of 3D Modeling

SolidWorks is utilized by Designers, Inventors, Students, Engineers, and other specialists to harvest simple and complex parts, assemblies, and drawings. Designing in a modeling software such as

SolidWorks is valuable because it minimizes our effort, money and saves time, that would else be spent prototyping the project.

System Requirements

For system requirements, see the SOLIDWORKS Website:

System requirements

http://www.solidworks.com/sw/support/SystemRequirements.html

Graphics requirements

http://www.solidworks.com/sw/support/videocardtesting.html

3D Design

- SOLIDWORKS usages a 3D project approach. As you design a part, from the initial sketch to the ending result, you make a 3D model. Since this model, you able to make 2D drawings or mate components containing of parts or sub-assemblies to generate 3D assemblies. You can likewise produce 2D sketches of 3D assemblies.

- Once planning a model with SOLIDWORKS, you can imagine it in three dimensions, the way the model happens when it is manufactured.

SOLIDWORKS 3D part   SOLIDWORKS 3D assembly

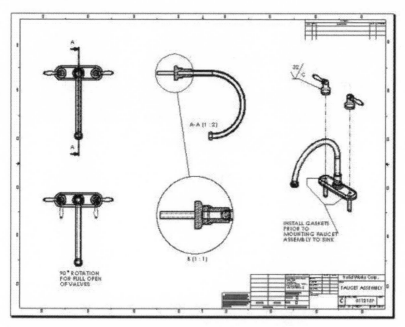

SOLIDWORKS 2D drawing generated from 3D model

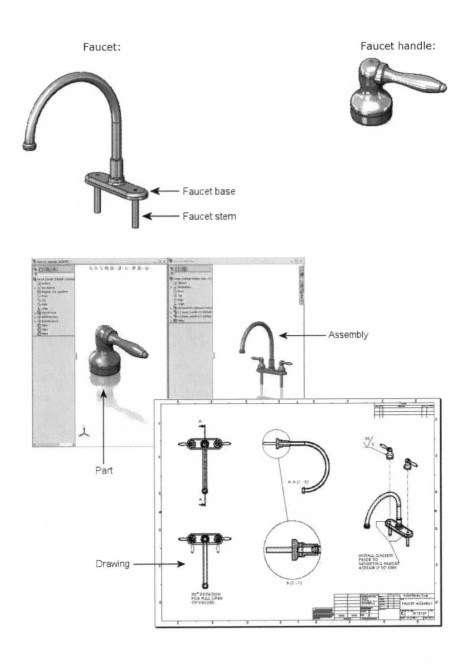

Faucet:

Faucet handle:

Faucet base

Faucet stem

Assembly

Part

Drawing

This section uses the following **terminology** for the models:

1.Plane, 2. Origin, 3. Axis, 4. Edge, 5. Face, 6. Vertex.

File Formats

Type	Function	Data File
Part	3-D Object	*.SLDPRT
Assembly	Many Parts	*.SLDASM
Drawing	Multi-views	*.SLDDRW

e.g.,
  Base.sldprt
  Base-Rod.sldasm
  Base.slddrw

Fundamentals of Solidworks

(2) 3-D Object Creation Procedure
By Creating Features

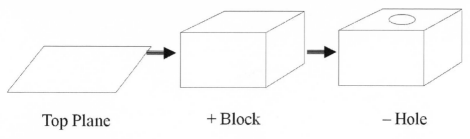

Top Plane   + Block   − Hole

Each Feature:
• 2-D Sketching
• 3-D Formation

(3) 2-D Sketching

Parametric Modeling

(a) Procedure

• Sketch the geometry

• Dimension the geometry

• Modify the dimension values

e.g.,

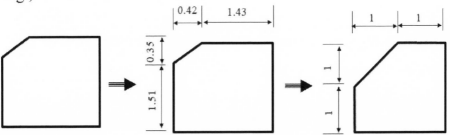

(b) 2-D Object Creation Methods

Menu: Tools->Sketch Entities

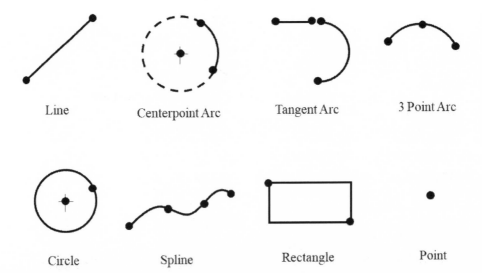

| Line | Centerpoint Arc | Tangent Arc | 3 Point Arc |

| Circle | Spline | Rectangle | Point |

(c) Additional 2-D Object Creation Methods
Menu: Tools->Sketch Tools

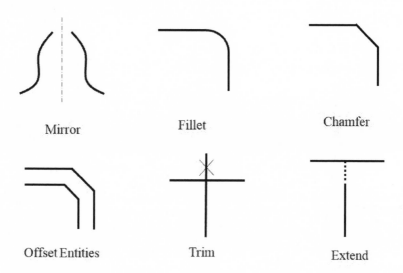

| Mirror | Fillet | Chamfer |

| Offset Entities | Trim | Extend |

(d) Dimensioning
Menu: Tools->Dimensions->Smart

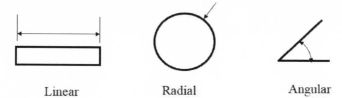

Linear   Radial   Angular

(e) Relations
Menu: Tools->Relations

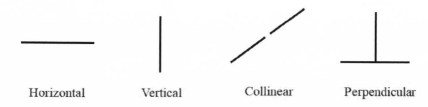

Horizontal   Vertical   Collinear   Perpendicular

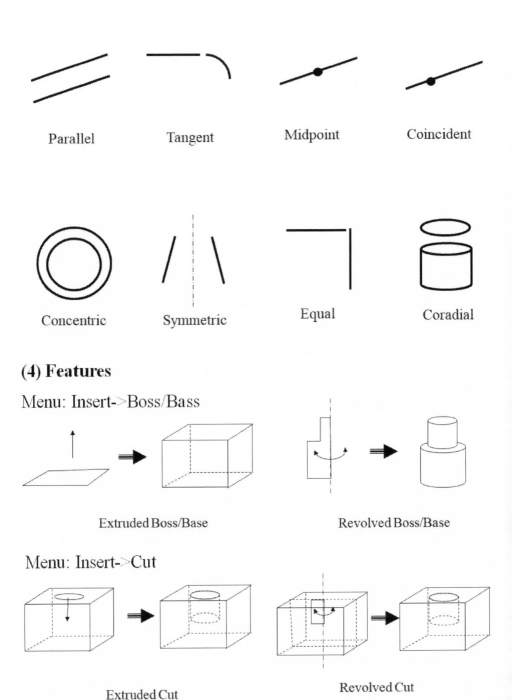

Parallel   Tangent   Midpoint   Coincident

Concentric   Symmetric   Equal   Coradial

(4) Features

Menu: Insert->Boss/Bass

Extruded Boss/Base   Revolved Boss/Base

Menu: Insert->Cut

Extruded Cut   Revolved Cut

Menu: Insert->Boss/Bass

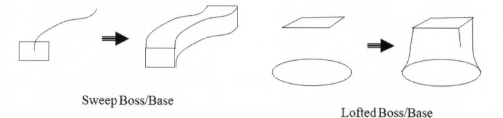

Sweep Boss/Base

Lofted Boss/Base

Menu: Insert->Features

Fillet

Chamfer

Menu: Insert->Pattern/Mirror

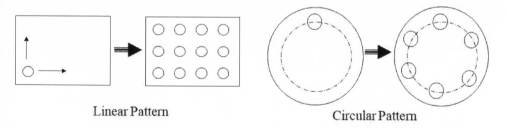

Linear Pattern

Circular Pattern

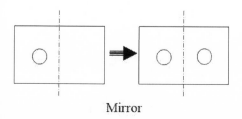

Mirror

(5) Reference Geometry

Menu: Insert->Reference Geometry

Plane   Axis   Coordinate System

e.g.,

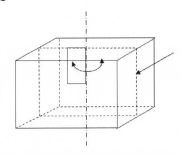

A reference plane for creating a sketch of revolved cut feature

(6) Viewing

Menu: View->Display

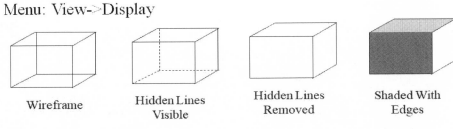

Wireframe   Hidden Lines Visible   Hidden Lines Removed   Shaded With Edges

Menu: View->Modify

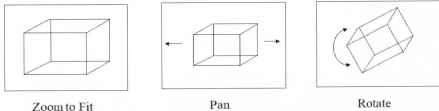

Zoom to Fit   Pan   Rotate

Assembly Modeling

(1) Loading the Apparatuses

Choose Menu: Insert->Component ->Existing Part/Assembly

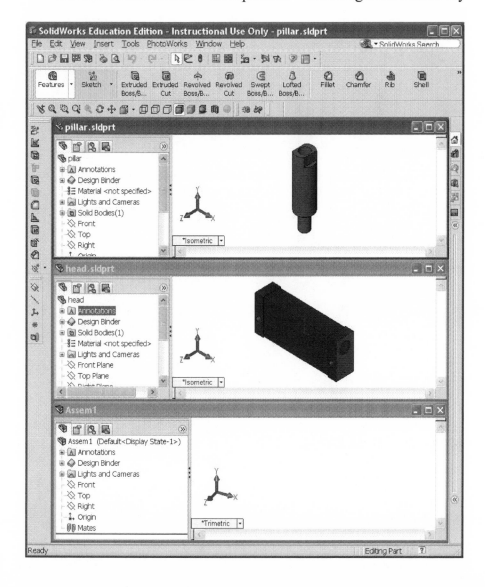

(2) Defining the Mates

Choose Menu: Insert->Mate

Coincident. Positions selected faces, edges, and planes (in combination with each other or combined with a single vertex) so they share the same infinite plane. Positions two vertices so they touch.

Parallel. Places the selected items so they remain a constant distance apart from each other.

Perpendicular. Places the selected items at a 90° angle to each other.

Tangent. Places the selected items tangent to each other (at least one selection must be a cylindrical, conical, or spherical face).

Concentric. Places the selections so that they share the same center line.

Distance. Places the selected items with the specified distance between them.

Angle. Places the selected items at the specified angle to each other.

(3) Exploded Views of model

Choose Menu: Insert->Exploded View

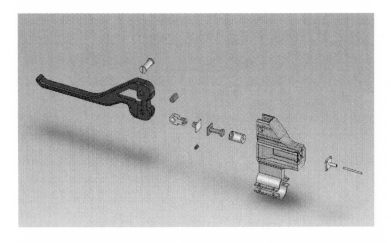

4. Draw Modeling

Two Dimension Drawing of a Part or an Assembly

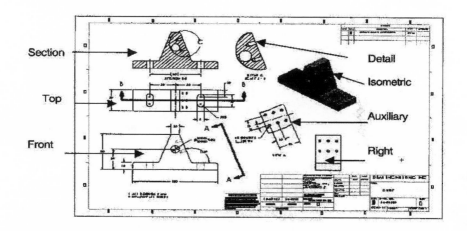

Solidworks Drawing Format and Template

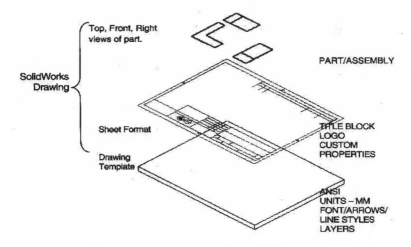

(Since 2003, source from the Planchard)

Drawing Formats

Choose Menu: File->New->Draw

Format Template Positioning

- Portrait

- Landscape

Template Size

- A4

- A3

- A

- B

Creating Views of Drawing

Select Menu: Insert->Drawing View

- There are 3 Standard View

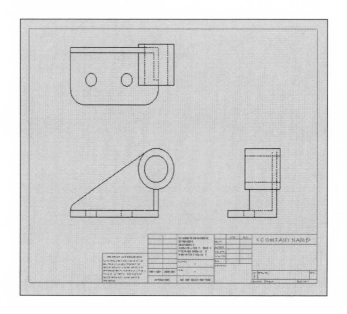

Model View in Orientation

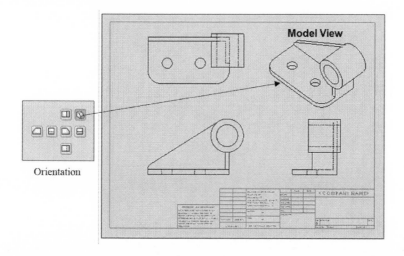

Solidworks Drawing Derived Views

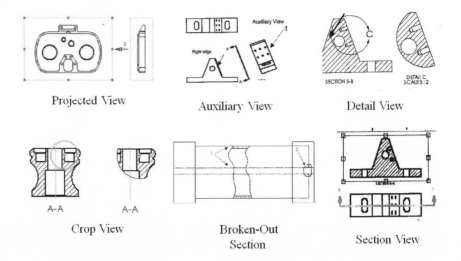

Projected View   Auxiliary View   Detail View

Crop View   Broken-Out Section   Section View

(3) Dimensions of Models

Choose Menu: Tools->Options

Choose Styles of Arrow, Font, Precision, Leader, Tolerance, etc.

Two Methods to set Dimensions

(i) Show All Dimensions and Before Modify Dimensions

Choose Menu: Insert->Model Items

(ii) Set Essential Dimensions Yourself.

Choose Menu: Tools->Dimensions

(4) Annotations

Menu: Insert->Annotations

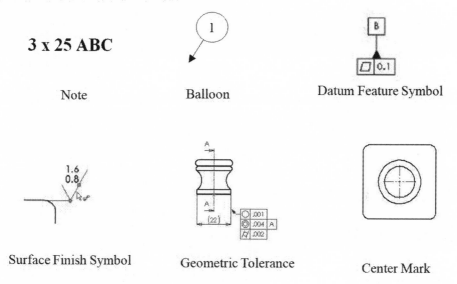

3 x 25 ABC	1	B / 0.1
Note	Balloon	Datum Feature Symbol
Surface Finish Symbol	Geometric Tolerance	Center Mark

(5) Solidworks Bill of Materials

Choose Menu: Insert->Tables->Bill of Materials

CHAPTER 2

SolidWorks – Let's start

- ➢ By defaulting, once you start the program no model opened repeatedly.
- ➢ To make a new model file, click on **File** in menu-bar > **New** or click the **New File icon** in the toolbar.
- ➢ Then automatically open the New SolidWorks File wizard.

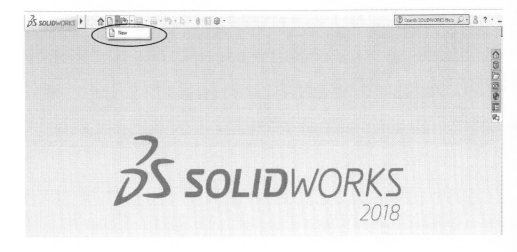

PARTS

 Part    Assembly    Drawing

- ➢ The primary and most important element of a SolidWorks model is a **Part.**

- Part contains of primitive geometry and features such as **revolutions, extrudes, sweeps, lofts,** etc.
- Parts is most vital **building blocks** for all of the prototypes which you will build.

ASSEMBLIES

- The another significant component is the **assembly**. Assemblies are **groups of parts** which are assembled in a specific fashion using mates (constraints).
- Any complex model will typically consist of one, or many assemblies.

DRAWINGS

- The 3rd and last component in SolidWorks is the **Drawing.**
- A drawing is the general way to **represent a 3D model** like that any product designer, manufacturer, or engineer can reconstruct your part.
- Drawings are significant because they make available a standard method of sharing your ideas or design.

SolidWorks Menu Tour

Let's start by making a new part. Toward do this, click on the **Part**, then OK, after you make sure of this, you will be carried into the modeling view that must open some toolbars and panes

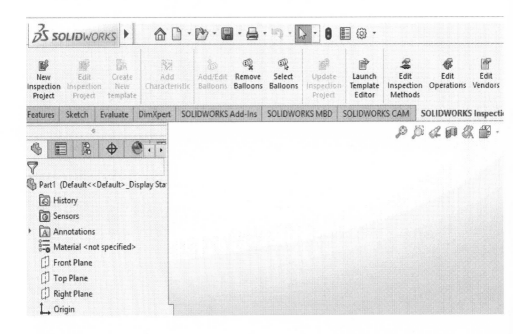

There are some important parts of the screen which wants to be known before we continue.

First, the left-side of the screen contains of some tabbed panes which provide very significant info about your model.

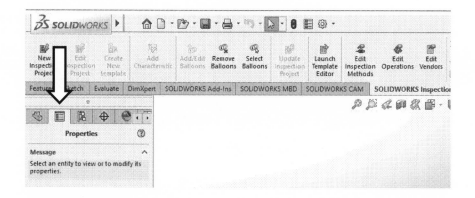

The 2nd Tab, so-called the **Property Manager**, permits you to alter the properties of different entities also during creation, or after that it will be created.

Note which is commonly you will don't want to physically change the tab on the manager window

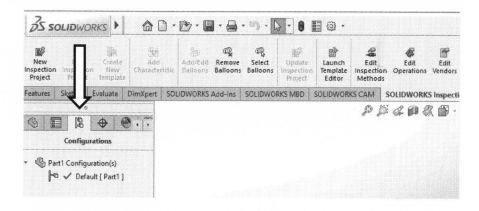

The 3rd Tab is named the **Configuration Manager** and is utilized to set-up dissimilar view configurations such as exploded views or 3D section views.

Typically, this has been used after the part has been created as well as you wish to set-up particular patterns for visualization.

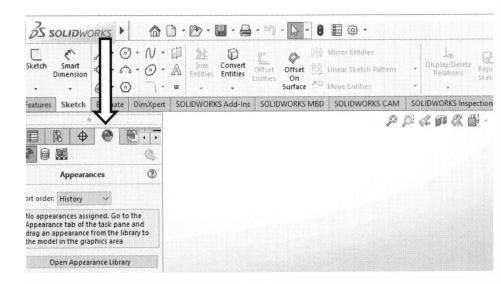

At this point, may well also be other tabs **visible in the manager**
window, Usually, anytime you load an extra SolidWorks module
(For Examples, COSMOS Motion, PhotoWorks, COSMOS Works,
etc.) this will be make a new tab in this window

Useful Websites (For Download Solidworks 3D Models)

- https://www.grabcad.com
- https://www.cadtek.com
- https://www.3Dcontentcentral.com
- https://www.turbosquid.com
- https://www.free3D.com

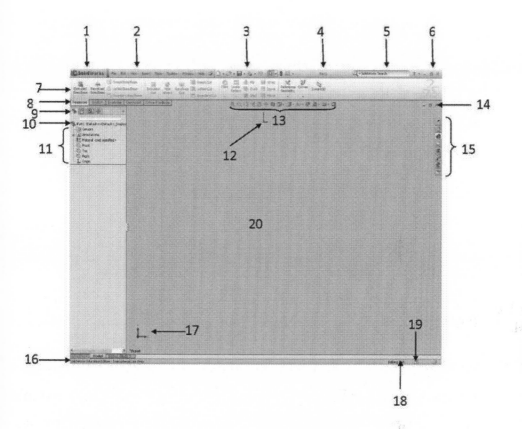

Table 1.1 – SolidWorks Desktop for a New Part Document

1- SolidWorks logo

2- Main Drop-down Menu

3- Quick Access Toolbar (also called the Standard Toolbar)

4- File name

5- SolidWorks search

6- Help (?) & Minimize/Maximize/Close window (see also 14)

7- CommandManager

8- CommandManager toolbars tabs

9- Feature/Property/Configuration managers tabs

10- File name

11- FeatureManager Design Tree (also called the Feature Tree)

12- Origin (red or blue)

13- View (Heads-Up) toolbar

14- Minimize/Maximize/Close window (see also 6)

15- Task pane

16- SolidWorks command description

17- Reference triad

18- SolidWorks status bar & units selection

19- Quick tips

20- Graphics area

Dynamic Toolbar

➢ The next significant appearance of the interface is the Dynamic Toolbar

➢ The Dynamic Toolbar provides the maximum relevant tools to access, and regularly using commands in SolidWorks.

➢ The final part of the interface and that should be well-known is the **Task Pane** on the right-side of the window.

➢ Using the Task Pane, you can able to view content specific tasks for example, file explorer, importing standard geometry, view palette, along with any plugin specific info.

➢ The last thing in order that want to be exposed is how to open the SolidWorks tutorials.

➢ They can be opened by going to **Help > SolidWorks Tutorials.**

➢ The instructions are valuable and cover from the most basic features to added advanced analysis and assemblies

This table lists the tools you use in the lesson and their positions on **menus, toolbars**, and the **Command Manager**.

Tool	Icon	Menu	Toolbar	CommandManager
New		File > New	Standard	Menu Bar
Save		File > Save	Standard	Menu Bar
Options		Tools > Options	Standard	Menu Bar
Sketch		Insert > Sketch	Sketch	Sketch
Smart Dimension		Tools > Dimensions > Smart	Sketch	Sketch
Rectangle		Tools > Sketch Entities > Rectangle	Sketch	Sketch
Extruded Boss/Base		Insert > Boss/Base > Extrude	Features	Features
Shell		Insert > Features > Shell	Features	Features
Insert Components		Insert > Component > Existing Part/Assembly	Assembly	Assembly
Mate		Insert > Mate	Assembly	Assembly

CHAPTER 3

Shaping and Joining

➢ Here and now in order that we have explored the interface of SolidWorks, let's make a simple part step-by-step.

➢ For here and now, we are simply going to concern ourselves with one type of feature: **Extruded Boss/Base.**

Why Extrude?

Extrude – Once you take a two-dimension space and press the design-out into additional dimension. A 2D space, such as, able to be complete into a three Dimension volume through extruding it out a particular distance, d.

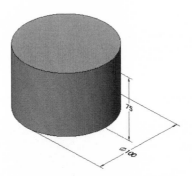

You able to extrude to create a **SOLID** or you able to extrude to create a **CUT**

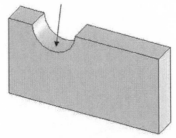

There are MANY ways to EXTRUDE a surface

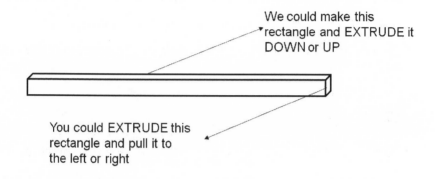

We could make this
rectangle and EXTRUDE it
DOWN or UP

You could EXTRUDE this
rectangle and pull it to
the left or right

Let's begin. Select FILE, then NEW PART

Shaping and Joining: Let's Begin

Initially, we are going to create a hollow semi sphere by mounting holes (as displayed). This will be done to announce you **to Extruding, Filleting, Shelling,** and **Extrusion Cutting.**

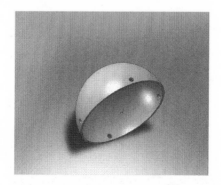

Opening a new Part

- By Opening a **New** model file in SolidWorks and selecting **Part** a screen alike the one display should appear.
- Since this 3D objects can be formed

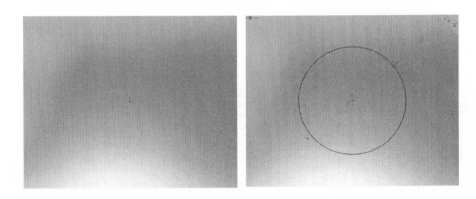

Example 1

Hollow semi sphere

- For making a new **part**, just click **sketch**, and then select **circle** along the task-bar.

- Choose the **front-plane** once the planes appear.

- Draw an arbitrary circle

- Use **Smart Dimensions** to appearance size (either right-click on the circle or usage the button on the top toolbar)

- Double-click over the size and change to 100mm (Left menu bar)

  - Click **Feature** on the task-bar.

  - Click **Extruded Bose/Base**

- Set size (D1) to 50mm

- Click the green tick (or press enter)

- Click Fillet on the task-bar

- Change radius to 50mm

- Click top-face of cylinder

- Press Enter in the keyboard

- Go to back of semi sphere (click then **back**)

- Click **Shell** on **Features** toolbar, now click the back-face

- Choose a shelling of 2mm and press enter

- Here, we will make 4 mounting holes in the side of the sphere.

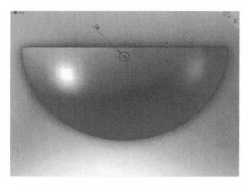 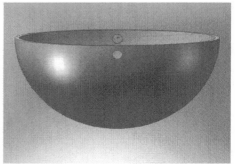

- Right click over the top-plane on the left-hand panel, choose insert sketch.

- Draw a 5mm diameter circle in the midpoint of the sphere (a dashed line will appear if you are centred).

- Create this 5mm from the edge (using smart dimensions).

- Now click the features button and choice **extruded cut** and, over the left-panel, through all instead of blind, use the **rotation tool** to see that it is going through the form, if not tick the arrows alongside through all to adjust the cut direction.

- Repeat for the right plane to produce 4 mounting holes

- Congratulations, you now know **Shelling, Extruding, Filleting** and **Extrusion Cutting.**

Make Sure You Save Your Work

- Through yourself make a 'new sketch' with a 96mm diameter semi sphere and some base.

Assembly

- In this segment of the outline we are going-to assemble the two previous components into one part.

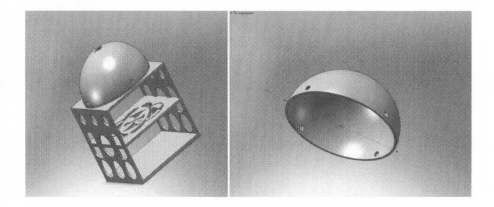

- Make a **new** SolidWorks **Assembly** Sheet.
- Click **Insert -> Component -> Existing Part**
- In the left, if your part is not there, click **Browse** and discover your part. Open it. (Note it will be there uncertainty the part is open in SolidWorks).

Adding Parts

- Now insert your second part the similar way
- Move the second part away from the additional (use Move component if needed)

Joining Parts

• Rotate your object using rotate component so that they face same ways – see figure (*note that you cannot change the first one you placed*).

• Click the **mate** tool (the paper clip)

• Choose the sphere rim, and a parallel surface to align the components

• Change the join from **coincident** to **parallel** click ok (else it might be joint in the wrong place!).

Note you might want

To rotate your screen to select both, use the rotation following to the magnifying glasses

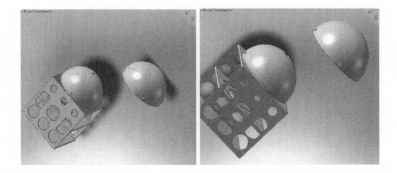

- Now choose connection hole internal face of both surfaces to align the holes (see figure, you might have-to zoom into get the face, not the edge – use the mouse scroll). Click OK.

- Finally select the internal sphere and external sphere of the top and bottom bits respectively to join the parts. Select OK two times to exit mating

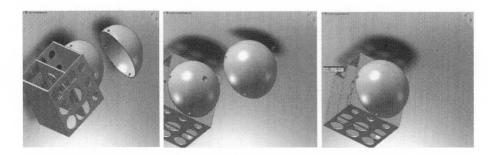

Checking design

- It is well practice to make sure the parts are not overlapping, so click **tools – Interference Detection – Calculate**.

- Any overlapping will be exposed, this means you haven't aligned the parts correctly or your measurements are wrong, the parts do not fit together!

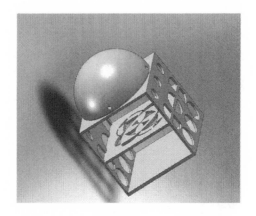

Exploding

- Occasionally it is valuable to see how the parts are joining together – this is anywhere the Exploded interpretation comes in.
- Select **Exploded View** in the Assemblies Toolbar
- Click the top of your assembly
- Click the **Blue** arrow and drag up (opposite pointed way in last slide)
- Click OK.
- Here and now by right-clicking on you project name (in left toolbar) you can choose **Collapse** or **Explode** to change between the two.

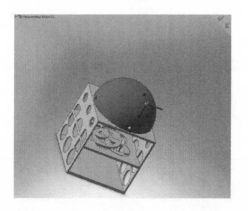

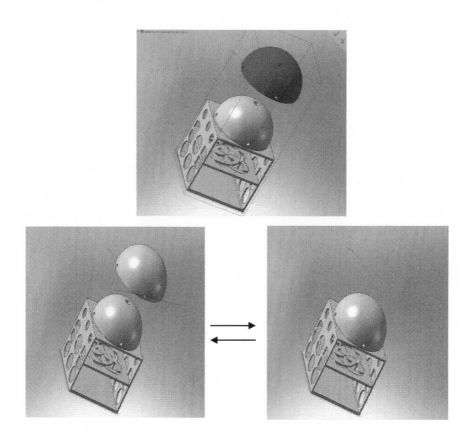

Section Cut

- At the top right of the window there is be a button like ▦
- Choose this and choice a plane to cut over on the left-hand-side (*note you be able to do this in the exploded or collapsed views*).

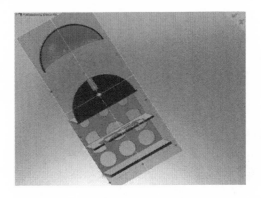

- Select OK to render this system, to exit this view just click the button again.

CHAPTER 4

Making a 3D Automoblox Car

- **Step1: Choose the "Front-Plane"** for make a new **sketch**
- Make a "**Center Rectangle**" beginning the origin of Smart Dimension Enter the length & width in inches

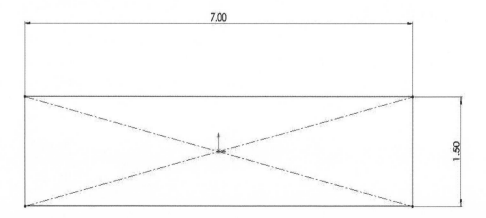

Step 2: Modification the View

- Modify the view to "Trimetric"
- Try middle-click on mouse and drag to freely rotate model

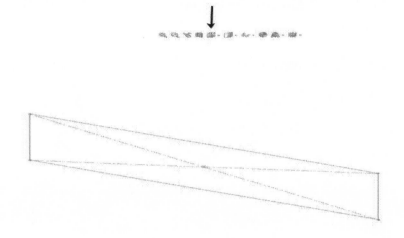

Step 3: Extrude the Centre Rectangle

- Select **Extrude** the sketch
- Select "**Mid Plane**", and set to 3.130"

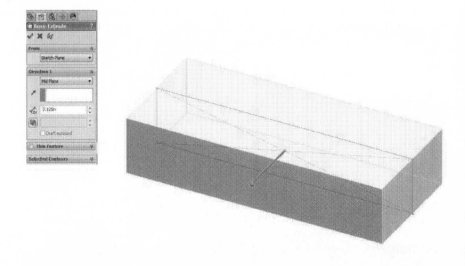

Step 4: Altering the Sketch

- Remove the extruded feature (we will come-back to in order that later)
- Then Edit the sketch; and draw a horizontal line under the box
- Set the line as "for construction"
- Dimension the line 0.280" under the box

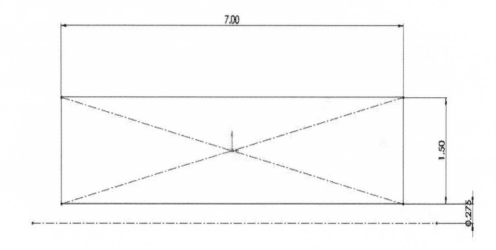

Step 5: Sketching the Wheel

Go to menu-bar and select circle as well as Draw a circle, linking the edge to the creation line so it is tangent

Dimension of the circle 1 inch away from the opposite Dimension, the diameter as 40mm (note, this one change to inches)

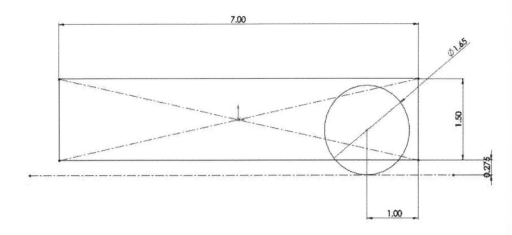

Step 6: New Sketch

Make a new sketch on the "**Front-plane**" and use "Convert Entities"

Then Choose the rectangle to convert (this accept it to the new sketch)

Extrude the box just as beforehand, by "Mid-Plane" & 3.130"

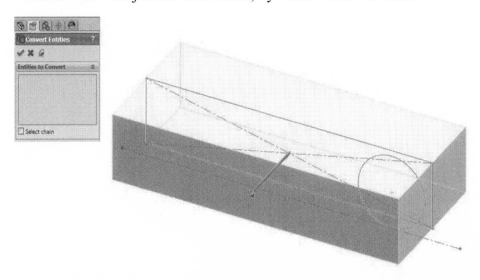

Step 7: Reference Plane

From the top menu, Select: these "Insert > Reference Geometry > Plane" enter the plane 0.20 or 0.10 inch away from the box face

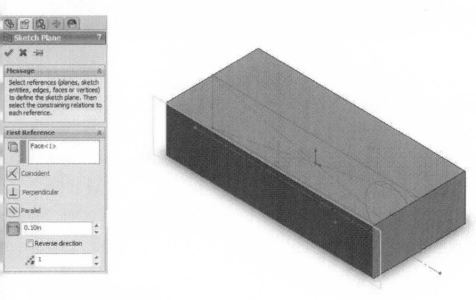

Step 8: New Sketch

Next step is Make a new sketch along the new reference plane and another time Use "Convert Entities".

Choice the circle to get it on this different sketch

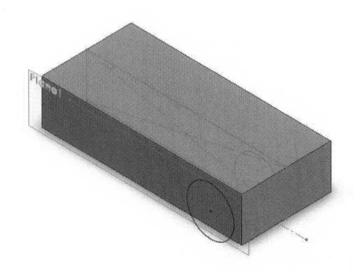

Step 9: Extrude the wheel

Next step is select circle and **Extrude the wheel**

Enter the dimension extrude as "Blind" and to 0.65"

Uncheck the box for "Merge result" as your needs,

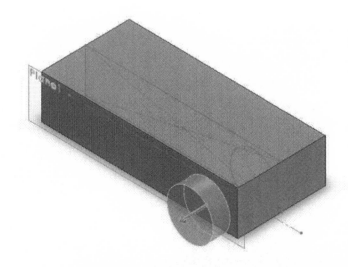

Step 10: Round the Corners

10th step is Choose the "Fillet" tool

Choose the edges of the box to fillet and enter the radius to 0.35"

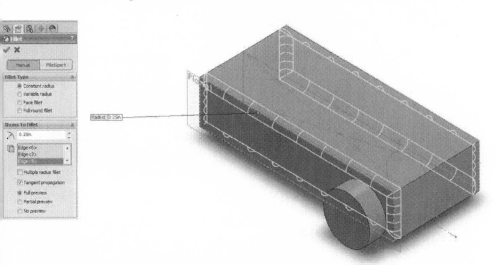

Step 11: Round the Edges of the Wheels

11th step is choosing the "Fillet" tool

Choose the edges of the wheel to fillet and enter the radius to 0.135"

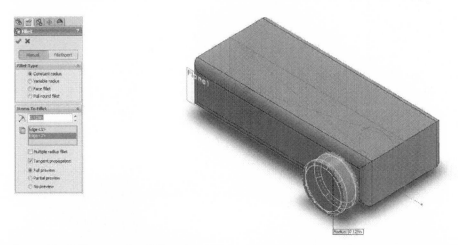

Step 12: Mirror the Wheels

- Choose the "Mirror" tool

- Then Select to mirror nearby the "Front-Plane"

- Go to "Bodies to Mirror", now click over the wheel in

- The model window

- (You be able to check preview to see what will occur)

 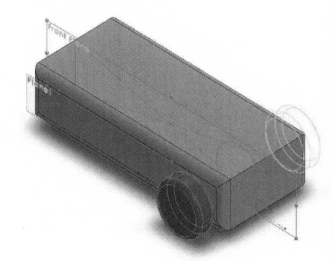

Step 13: Mirror the Wheels

- Repeat the before steps for another wheel

- Choose the "Mirror" tool again

- Select toward mirror nearby the "Right-plane"

- Then Go to "Bodies to Mirror", and now
  click over the two wheels in the model
  window

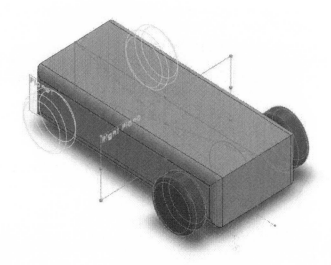

Step 14: Sketch the Canopy

Make a new sketch along the "Front-Plane"

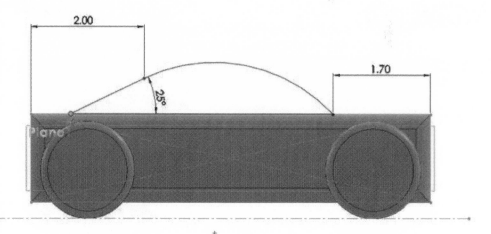

- Then **Sketch a line** along the top edge of car (but, by not the entire car)

- Sketch a line close to one end of initial and have it near an angle

- Dimension the lines with 1.80 or 1.70", 2.00", and angle of 30° or 25° (you can change the dimension as you need)
- Draw a tangent arc to the right-angled line and finish on the right, by end of the initial line
- (Similarly, try dragging nearby the point over the left to modify the shape of the canopy)

Step 15: Extrude the Canopy

Extrude the canopy

Use "Mid-Plane" and enter to 2.30"

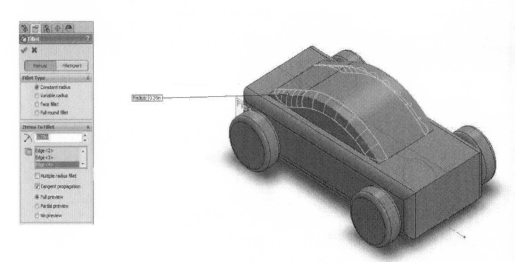

Fillet the upper edges of the canopy to 0.40"

Step 16: Hide the Body

Right-click over the feature for the car body, as
well as select "Hide" to create it invisible

Rotate the view to see the base of the canopy

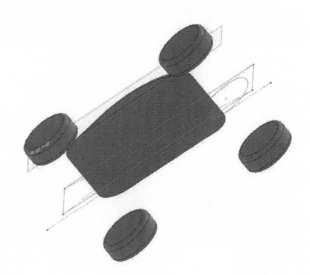

Step 17: Shell the Canopy

Choose the "Shell" tool

Enter the shell thickness to 0.15 or 0.10"

(Attention: just how this hollows out the canopy)

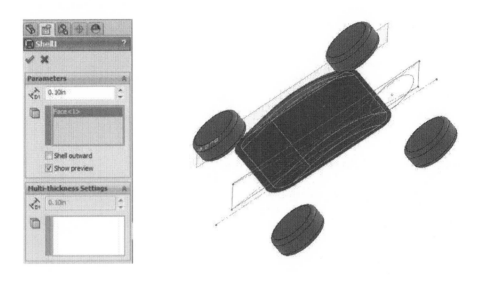

Step 18: Glass Canopy

Final step Flip the car back about using "Isometric" as well as Create the car body visible again by right-clicking, then "Edit the Appearance" to create it extra realistic

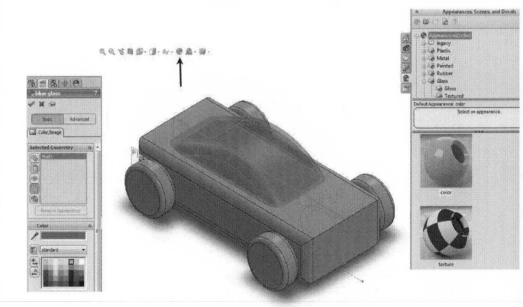

Other things to try...

- Try changing the original rectangle for this car body to create it better match the Automoblox cars
- What happens once you modify the dimension for the "ground clearance" construction line?
- Try addition a spoiler or other part
- Make axles and corresponding holes for the wheels

Keyboard Short-cut Commands

Keyboard Commands are shortcuts you can utilizing to as a replacement for the clicking icons on the Toolbars.

Category	Command	Shortcut(s)
File	New..	Ctrl+N
File	Open..	Ctrl+O
File	Close..	Ctrl+W
File	Save..	Ctrl+S
File	Print..	Ctrl+P
File	Browse Recent Documents..	R
Edit	Undo..	Ctrl+Z
Edit	Redo..	Ctrl+Y
Edit	Repeat Last Command..	Enter
Edit	Cut..	Ctrl+X
Edit	Copy..	Ctrl+C
Edit	Paste..	Ctrl+V
Edit	Delete..	Delete
Edit	Rebuild..	Ctrl+B
View	Redraw..	Ctrl+R
View	Orientation..	SpaceBar
View	Zoom to Fit..	F
View	Quick Snaps..	F3
View	Full Screen..	F11
View	FeatureManager Tree Area..	F9
View	Toolbars..	F10
View	Task Pane..	Ctrl+F1
Tools	Line..	L
Others	Front	Ctrl+1
Others	Back	Ctrl+2
Others	Left	Ctrl+3
Others	Right	Ctrl+4
Others	Top	Ctrl+5
Others	Bottom	Ctrl+6
Others	Isometric	Ctrl+7
Others	Normal To	Ctrl+8
Others	Command option toggle	A
Others	Expand/Collapse Tree	C
Others	Collapse all Items..	Shift+C
Others	Filter Edges	E
Others	Find/Replace	Ctrl+F
Others	Next Edge	N
Others	Force Regen	Ctrl+Q
Others	Magnifying Glass	G
Others	Shortcut Bar	S
Others	Filter Vertices	V
Others	Toggle Selection Filter Toolbar	F5
Others	Toggle Selection Filters	F6
Others	Spell Checker	F7
Others	Filter Faces	X
Others	Accept Edge	Y
Others	Zoom Out	Z
Others	Zoom In	Shift+Z
Others	Previous View	Ctrl+Shift+Z

Feature based Comparison of AUTODESK INVENTOR vs SOLIDWORKS

SOLIDWORKS and Inventor are two of the main **Three-dimension CAD modeling** stages, used in the greater part of the ventures today. With each having its exact own separating factors, there is dependably an inquiry on picking the one that is ideal. While some incline toward the ease of use of SOLIDWORKS, some discover Inventor as a superior choice to suit particular prerequisites. Looking at the two anyway resembles contrasting apples Versus apples. Both are similarly able to help design engineers to model complex geometries easily and have their very own modules or features incorporated to expand the design for different divisions.

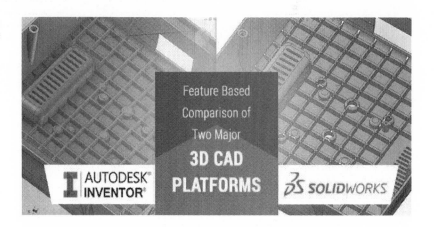

At Hi-Tech, we were using both these tools for our customers. Dealing with various projects including sheet metal, solid modeling, extensive assemblies, design automation and 3D rendering, we feel that there are sure critical features that can unquestionably separate these two driving CAD modeling stages. Here are some of them:

Sketch :		
Function	**AUTODESK® INVENTOR®**	**ⅅ꒰ SOLIDWORKS**
Contour	Closing the contour finishes the line automatically	Requires pressing ESC to finish the line
Dimensioning Tool	Less functionality and requires additional click for aligned dimension	Advanced functions such as text formatting, symbols, comments, etc.
Editing	Changing the geometry size causes instability at times	Remains stable
Sketch Constraints	Less User Friendly	More User Friendly

Features:		
Function	**AUTODESK® INVENTOR®**	**ⅅ꒰ SOLIDWORKS**
Extrude	Reference must be surface to start or end extrude	Can be vertex, surface or offset from surface
Revolve	Reference for "To" must be surface and no possibility to Offset for "From" reference	It is possible to reference vertex for both "To" and "From"
Hole Wizard	**End Condition:** Distance, Through all, To **Slots:** No **Hole on Curved Face:** Additional plane required	**End Condition:** Blind, Through all, Up to Next, Up to Vertex, Up to Surface and Offset from Surface **Slots:** Yes **Hole in Curved Face:** Can be placed on any face
Sweep	**Profile Twist:** Limited possibility **Bidirectional Sweep:** Not available	**Profile Twist:** Greater possibility **Bidirectional Sweep:** Yes
Patterns	**Linear/Rectangular:** Yes but not possible to skip instances **Circular:** Yes, but cannot skip instances. More options in positioning method.	**Linear/Rectangular:** Yes **Circular:** Yes. Only linear positioning method available. **Other Patterns:** Sketch driven, Curve driven, Table driven, Fill pattern.

Assemblies:

Function	AUTODESK® INVENTOR®	DS SOLIDWORKS
Mates/Joints	Standard Mates: Coincident, Parallel, Perpendicular, Concentric, Distance, Angle Width Mate: No Mechanical Mates: Few	Standard Mates: Coincident, Parallel, Perpendicular, Concentric, Distance, Angle Width Mate: Yes Mechanical Mates: More advances
Assembly Inspection	Interference detection	Interference detection, clearance verification, hole alignment
Large Assemblies	**Load Modes:** Resolved and Express	**Load Modes:** Resolved, Lightweight, Large Assembly Mode and Large Design Review

Drawings:

Function	AUTODESK® INVENTOR®	DS SOLIDWORKS
Printing	Drawings sheets can be excluded from printing or counting	No such possibility
Update Drawing	"Defer Updates" function to stop updating drawing from the model	No such possibility
Dimension Favorites	Not available	Available. It is also possible to add text under dimension line

When the comparison couldn't be comprehensive, it is obviously noticeable which SOLIDWORKS offers significantly more usefulness with each element to save design process without glitch. That being stated, Inventor still takes various features that come by way of standard contrasted with the essential SOLIDWORKS rendition. +

Also, Inventor has important cost efficient of ownership. Both the stages have design automation ability. While Inventor uses an in-assembled iLogic highlight, SOLIDWORKS utilizes an outsider arrangement called DriveWorksXpress which is free however has constrained usefulness. For a complete building design automation and CAD customization arrangement, it is required to buy Solo or Pro form of the DriveWorks.

How to Download Popular Soldworks Model from the Internet.

Step1: Go To the Website https://grabcad.com/library

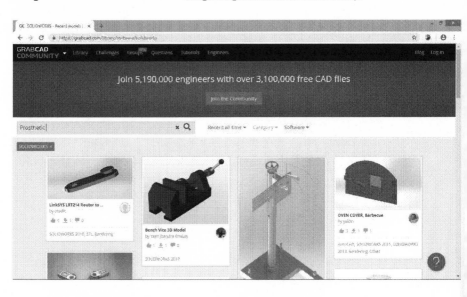

There, you will have seen more than 3 Million CAD Files from the 5 Million Engineers

Step 2: Search the models name, what you need, and download it.

Step 3: Extract the zip file

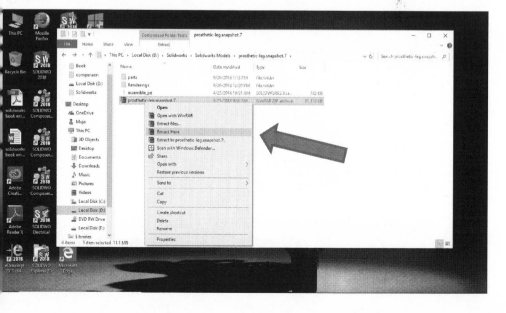

Step 4: Double Click to open Assemble or part file

Name	Date modified	Type	Size
parts	9/26/2018 1:13 PM	File folder	
Renderings	9/26/2018 12:20 PM	File folder	
assemble_pé	4/22/2014 10:51 AM	SOLIDWORKS Ass...	742 KB
prosthetic-leg.	6 PM	WinRAR ZIP archive	11,376 KB

Type: LIDWORKS Assembly Document

Step 5: Finally download model will be appearing, you can able to edit and recreate solid anytime, press and hold the scroll button in mouse for 360 Degree Rotation.

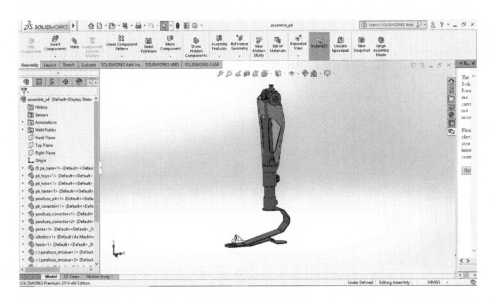

Important Internet Resources (Best Links)

Solidworks Tutorials (Best Video Tutorials ZERO to HERO)

https://www.youtube.com/channel/UCtwaWPOXEBysZLh1rrPzwFw

CAD and CAM Tutorials (Best Video Tutorials for CAD & CAM)

https://www.youtube.com/channel/UCjd_zIvYtQymk0dPx3vTJcA

Tutorials Engineers: (Solidworks Complete Learning Video Tutorials)

https://www.youtube.com/playlist?list=PLkMYhICFMsGajeARsY7N1t1jhbtMb1poL

Skateboarding news: http://skateboard.about.com/

Website for Solidworks Tutorials Beginners

http://solidworkstutorialsforbeginners.com/solidworks-tutorials-for-beginners/

Beginners Guide for Solidworks http://www.solidworkstutorials.com

CADeducators.com website: http://www.cadeducators.com

CAD History: http://www.cadhistory.net/

CAD news and information:
http://www.caddigest.com/subjects/solidworks/index.htm

Skateboard design: http://en.wikipedia.org/wiki/Skateboard

Skateboarding science: http://exploratorium.edu/skateboarding/trick02.html

CADeducators.com website: http://www.cadeducators.com

SolidWorks website: http://www.solidworks.com

CAD Models for download: http://b2b.partcommunity.com/community/

Skateboarding history: http://en.wikipedia.org/wiki/Skateboarding

Click here for SolidWorks models free download:
http://www.3dcontentcentral.com/3dcontentcentral/

SolidWorks training files:
http://www.solidworks.com/sw/support/807_ENU_HTML.htm

Design tables and information: http://www.engineeringtoolbox.com/

SolidWorks models for download:
http://www.3dcontentcentral.com/3dcontentcentral/

Popular CAD models for download:
http://grabcad.com/library/software/solidworks

SolidWorks tutorials: http://www.solidworks.com/sw/resources/solidworks-tutorials.htm

Popular CAD models for download:
http://grabcad.com/library/software/solidworks

Solid Professor tutorials: http://www.solidprofessor.com/

Suppliers CAD models for download: http://cad.thomasnet.com/cadmodels.html

American National Standards Institute (ANSI) website: http://www.ansi.org

Polyurethane properties: http://www.polyurethanes.org/en/what-is-it

International Standards Organization (ISO) website: http://www.iso.org

Wikipedia.com: http://en.wikipedia.org/wiki/Engineering_drawing

NASA Technical Drawings: http://history.nasa.gov/diagrams/diagrams.htm

About The Author

Arsath Natheem is an Indian Biomedical Engineer and Youtuber who works primarily in the field of Artificial intelligence, He is best known for his multimedia Presentation about "How the Biomedical Engineers Save the life" at VCET in Tamilnadu, he was awarded the best project holder for Human Interaction Intelligence Robot as Personal Assistance, and IoT Based Voice Recognition Robot for defenses, also presented his project at Adhiyamaan CET and won the first prize for his project. He participated project competition at Madras institute of technology (MIT) in Chennai, He completed his Undergraduate Degree at VCET, His area of interest is Prosthetic Design and Developments that's will be specifically applicable for Rehabilitation.

One Last Thing…

If you enjoyed this book or found it useful I'd be very grateful if you'd post a short review on Amazon. Your support really does make a difference and I read all the reviews personally so I can get your feedback and make this book even better.

If you'd like to leave a review, then all you need to do is click the review link on this book's page on Amazon.com

Thanks again for your support!

Made in the USA
Coppell, TX
04 November 2019